Cornerstones of Freedom

The Capitol

Andrew Santella

CHILDRENS PRESS®
CHICAGO

Library of Congress Cataloging-in-Publication Data

Santella, Andrew.
  The Capitol/by Andrew Santella.
    p. cm.–(Cornerstones of freedom)
  ISBN 0-516-06626-9
  1. United States Capitol (Washington, D.C.)—Juvenile
literature. 2. Washington (D.C.)—Buildings, structures,
etc.—Juvenile literature. [1. United States Capitol
(Washington (D.C.)]
I. Title. II. Series.
F204.C2S26 1995
975.3—dc20   95-825
                                      CIP
                                       AC

The Capitol in Washington, D.C., is one of the most recognizable buildings in the world. Its splendid dome stands as a symbol of American democracy and self-government. The Capitol is where our elected representatives gather to make the laws by which we live. The great American writer Nathaniel Hawthorne once called the Capitol "the center and heart of America."

Construction on the Capitol began in 1793, when the United States was still a new nation. Over the next two hundred years, it was expanded, redesigned, and improved. After it was damaged by a fire, the Capitol was even rebuilt. Through the difficult years of the Civil War, construction continued on the Capitol's new dome. It served as a sign to Americans that the nation would endure.

Like American democracy itself, the Capitol building has been a work in progress. As the nation has changed and grown, the Capitol has grown with it. Today, the Capitol is more than 751 feet long and 350 feet wide. Its floor space covers over sixteen acres. At its highest point (the top of the statue *Freedom*), the Capitol is 287 feet tall. Inside, there are 850 doorways and 540 rooms, including chambers for the U.S. Senate and the U.S. House of Representatives.

The Capitol has been the site of some of the most important events in American history. After their deaths, many presidents have lain in state in the Capitol's great Rotunda. Nearly all the U.S. presidents since Andrew Jackson (in 1829) have been inaugurated on the Capitol steps. In 1835, an assassin attempted, but failed, to murder President Jackson as he was leaving the Capitol. In 1844, Samuel Morse first demonstrated his revolutionary invention, the telegraph, from the Capitol. He sent a message to his assistant, who was fifty miles away in Baltimore.

The body of President Dwight D. Eisenhower lies in state in the Capitol Rotunda in 1969.

5

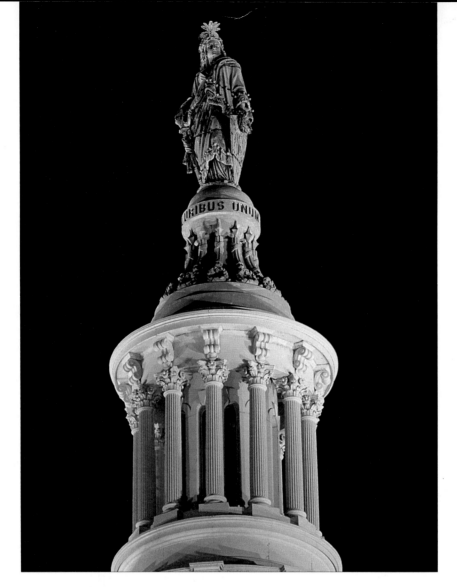

The statue Freedom *stands atop the Capitol dome. Inscribed at the base of the statue are the words* E Pluribus Unum.

At the base of the statue *Freedom* are inscribed the Latin words *E Pluribus Unum.* This means "Out of many, one." These words capture the spirit of the Capitol. It is here that representatives of all Americans meet to conduct the business of government. The work done by members of Congress ensures that the many different voices of the United States will be heard and will help shape a unified nation.

The story of the Capitol begins with the U.S. Constitution. In 1787, the writers of the Constitution allowed for a permanent home for the federal government, but they did not specify where this home would be established. After much debate, Congress finally passed the Residence Act in 1790. This law stated that the government would take residence on the banks of the Potomac River, between Virginia and Maryland. At the time, the nation's capital was New York City. The new capital city would be named Washington, in honor of the nation's first president and hero of the Revolutionary War.

This map, drawn in the 1790s, shows how architect Pierre Charles L'Enfant envisioned the street grid of the capital city. Just as L'Enfant designed it, the Capitol and the White House (called the President's House on this map) are both positioned along Pennsylvania Avenue in today's Washington, D.C.

Pierre Charles L'Enfant

Even though the Capitol is a historic American building, its first designer was a French engineer. The commissioners in charge of constructing new government buildings in Washington hired the talented French engineer Pierre Charles L'Enfant. They asked him to develop a plan for the new city, to design the important government buildings, and to oversee their construction.

L'Enfant produced an ambitious plan for Washington, D.C. It included grand plazas, public squares, and parks connected by wide boulevards. For the Capitol building, L'Enfant selected a site known as Jenkins Hill. He called it "a pedestal waiting for a monument." On a June morning in 1791, L'Enfant and President George Washington rode there on horseback. The president was impressed, and he urged L'Enfant to go forward with his plan. The stubborn L'Enfant, however, refused to produce an actual plan for the building, claiming he carried his ideas "in his head." L'Enfant had several other disagreements with the commissioners, and they

fired him in 1792.

The government now had to look for another architect to design its home. Secretary of State Thomas Jefferson, himself an amateur architect, suggested that the government hold a design competition. The architect with the best design would win the prize of $500 and a city lot. The competition drew at least sixteen entries. Some of the designs were quite imaginative. One showed a giant rooster weathervane crowing from the roof of the building. Although some of the designs were impressive, none were quite right for the future home of the United States government.

Several months after the competition deadline, a doctor from the British West Indies named William Thornton was allowed to submit his design. Although he made his living as a doctor, Thornton had a talent for painting and architecture. His design "captivated the eyes and judgment of all," said Jefferson. President Washington praised it for its "grandeur, simplicity, and convenience."

Thomas Jefferson

Opposite Page: One of the Capitol designs not chosen Below: William Thornton's winning design

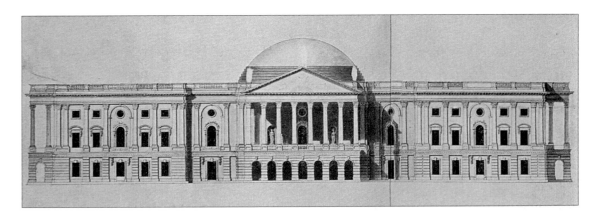

Thornton's design called for a domed central building that was modeled on the Pantheon, a famous temple of ancient Rome. Thornton designed two wings on each side of the building—one to house the Senate, and one for the House of Representatives.

Workmen began digging foundations for the Capitol in August 1793. On September 18, 1793, President Washington laid the cornerstone of the building and construction began. Work proceeded so slowly, however, that construction was continually behind schedule. To be lured from their homes to the new city of Washington, workers had to be paid higher wages than usual.

George Washington lays the cornerstone for the Capitol, a ceremony that marks the beginning of a building's construction.

The heavy sandstone used for some parts of the building had to be brought to the site by boat. Some boats were so overloaded that they sank on the way to the construction site. And the builders were continually running short of money to fund the project.

Because of these and other problems, the commissioners had to halt construction and change their plans. In 1796, they decided to abandon work on the domed center building and South Wing that Thornton had planned. Instead, they concentrated on completing the North Wing. With Congress scheduled to move into the Capitol in 1800, they reasoned that it would be better to have one completed wing than to have all three unfinished.

Even though William Thornton's design was very popular, the commissioners decided that a more experienced architect was needed to oversee the construction. They hired two architects, but both were immediately fired because they asked for too many changes to the design. Finally, a third architect, James Hoban, was brought in to complete this initial stage of building. (Hoban had designed the President's House, later called the White House, in 1792.)

By 1800, the North Wing of the Capitol was complete, except for some of the rooms on the third floor. The Senate, the House of Representatives, the Supreme Court, the Library of Congress, and the district courts all squeezed into their cramped new home. Congress convened there for the first time on November 21, 1800. The next day, President John Adams addressed Congress. He said he wanted to officially "congratulate the people of the United States on the assembling of Congress at their permanent seat of government."

For the 106 representatives and 32 senators gathered there, the building quickly became overcrowded. To ease the situation, they tried a number of temporary solutions. For instance, the House of Representatives met for several years in a different building. It was so stuffy and overheated that it was nicknamed "the Oven."

Fortunately, construction on the other permanent wings of the Capitol was continuing. In 1803, President Thomas Jefferson appointed Benjamin Latrobe architect of the Capitol. The same year, Congress set aside $50,000 to help speed construction of its new home. In 1807, Latrobe finally completed the South Wing, which included his magnificent Hall of the House, where the House of Representatives would meet. President Jefferson and others praised Latrobe's work, but some critics were not impressed. Representative John Randolph of Virginia complained that echoes in the Hall of the House made it almost impossible to hear speakers.

Benjamin Henry Latrobe was the second person appointed to the position of architect of the Capitol; the first was William Thornton. In the country's early years, the architect of the Capitol was responsible for overseeing the construction and expansion of the Capitol building, itself. In later years, the men who held this position also designed the buildings that house the Library of Congress, the Supreme Court, and the U.S. Botanic Garden, among many others.

Congress soon faced a crisis that would change the history of the young republic and its Capitol. The United States and Great Britain were engaged in a dispute because the British were unlawfully detaining American sailors. On June 18, 1812, Congress declared war on Great Britain. The conflict came to be known as the War of 1812.

For two years, the war was fought far from Washington. But in the summer of 1814, a British force landed in Maryland and marched to Washington. Not only did they capture the city, they burned most of it to the ground. The Capitol did not escape damage. Most of its interior was destroyed. However, a sudden rainstorm prevented the building from being completely burned down.

The British soon left the city, and by that fall Congress was again meeting in Washington— this time in a former hotel. For the next four years, Congress met in a quickly constructed building called the "Brick Capitol."

When Benjamin Latrobe came back to Washington and saw the damaged Capitol, he called it "a most magnificent ruin." He then set to work restoring the ruin.

Smoke-darkened stones were scrubbed clean. Those that were beyond rescue were replaced. The House Chamber was redesigned, and the Senate Chamber was enlarged and beautified. Latrobe could not make all the changes he wanted, however. When the commissioner of public buildings would not approve some of his plans for the Senate and House Chambers, Latrobe resigned in 1817.

The "Brick Capitol," the building where Congress met while the Capitol was repaired

Charles Bulfinch

The next year, Charles Bulfinch was hired to replace Latrobe as architect of the Capitol. Bulfinch immediately began working on the long-awaited center building that would finally connect the North and South wings. Both Thornton and Latrobe had left behind designs for the center building, but Bulfinch had his own ideas. His Rotunda, a large circular hall, was topped by a wooden dome covered in copper. In 1824, the Rotunda was opened. By 1826, after thirty-seven years of construction, the Capitol was complete.

An 1830s view of the Capitol's magnificent Rotunda

For the next twenty years, no major work was done on the Capitol. But the nation itself grew at an amazing rate. New states entered the Union, and the country's population nearly doubled between 1840 and 1860. As the population grew, so did the number of congressmen. By 1850, 62 senators and 232 representatives sat in Congress. The chambers they occupied were not designed to accommodate such large numbers. So Congress approved an expansion of the original wings of the Capitol.

The earliest known photograph of the Capitol, taken in 1846, shows the Rotunda topped with its old, wooden dome.

President Millard Fillmore appointed Thomas U. Walter architect of the Capitol in 1851. Walter's expansion doubled the size of the building by adding to the wings on either side of the center building. He designed new chambers for both the Senate and the House of Representatives. He beautified the interior of the Capitol. But the most visible change of all was the larger, cast-iron dome he designed to replace the old, wooden one.

The House moved into its new home in 1857 and the Senate took up its new residence in 1859. But even as these plans for the future moved forward, the nation was facing the worst crisis it ever encountered. The conflict between the southern and northern states threatened the very existence of the Union. In 1861, the Civil War began, pitting the South against the North.

At the beginning of the war, the Capitol was turned into a makeshift barracks for Union (northern) troops. They called their headquarters the "Big Tent." As many as 3,000 soldiers were quartered in the building at one time. Basement meeting rooms were turned into a bakery to supply bread for the troops. The Capitol was also used as an emergency hospital for the wounded.

As the war raged on, construction on the Capitol's new dome continued. President Abraham Lincoln was initially criticized for spending money on the dome while the nation

Construction equipment was visible at President Abraham Lincoln's first inauguration in 1861 (top). The wooden Capitol dome was being replaced with an iron dome (bottom).

was involved in a brutal war. But Lincoln defended himself, claiming that the Capitol dome was a symbol of national unity. "If the people see the Capitol [construction] going on," Lincoln said, "they will take it as a sign that the Union will go on." The same dome that was constructed during the Civil War tops the Capitol today. The dome is actually made of two fitted cast-iron shells. Together, they weigh nearly nine million pounds.

When the dome was finished in 1863, it was topped by the statue *Freedom*, the work of American artist Thomas Crawford. The enormous bronze figure is over nineteen feet tall. It stood throughout the last years of the Civil War and remains atop the Capitol today, fulfilling President Lincoln's vision.

Above: Thomas Crawford
Right: A design sketch for Crawford's statue Freedom

Since the Civil War, many modern facilities have been installed in the Capitol. Indoor plumbing was added in 1865, and by 1900 the Capitol had electricity in every room. Air conditioning was installed in 1929. Since the iron dome was added in 1863, however, there have been few major renovations to the exterior. In 1959, a new marble front was added to the east side of the building, about thirty-two feet east of the original sandstone wall. The alteration provided more space and gave the building a more balanced appearance.

Over the years, the federal government has outgrown the walls of the Capitol, which is in the center of this photograph. The two buildings to the left house the Library of Congress. The buildings to the right house the offices of the U.S. Senate. Offices for members of the House of Representatives are located in other buildings near the Capitol.

In 1976, a major restoration project was completed on the Capitol. As part of the country's 200th birthday celebration, the old House, Senate, and Supreme Court chambers were returned to their original condition. And from 1983 to 1987, the western exterior walls were cleaned, weatherproofed, and restored.

In the 1980s, the west front of the Capitol was restored and covered by marble. This was done because the old sandstone walls had deteriorated over the years.

Today, the Capitol operates in a way that would amaze the building's original designers of two centuries ago. The Capitol is almost a self-contained city, housing everything from a post office to barber shops and banks. The building even has its own power plant. Congress's 100 senators and 435 representatives travel to and from their office buildings on a private subway. They are protected by a special Capitol police force.

The magnificent view looking up from the floor of the Rotunda

Modern technology allows every U.S. citizen to "visit" the Capitol every day. Broadcasts of House and Senate sessions are carried on cable television in virtually every American community. And in 1995, the Library of Congress made available on the Internet the full text of all congressional acts and debates.

The Capitol building is open to visitors from across the nation and around the world. People walk through the magnificent Rotunda, which is home to many historic paintings and statues. Looking up, visitors see the interior of Thomas Walter's tremendous dome. The ceiling of the dome is covered with artist Constantino Brumidi's magnificent painting called *The Apotheosis of George Washington*. The painting covers 4,664 square feet, and depicts Greek gods and goddesses with famous figures from American history. For twenty-five years, Brumidi created numerous paintings and sculptures that still decorate the walls, ceilings, and corridors of the Capitol. Priceless works of many other artists make their home at the Capitol.

Italian-born artist Constantino Brumidi's spectacular painting The Apotheosis of George Washington, *which caps the interior of the dome*

Right: The walls and ceiling of this hallway are decorated with paintings of Constantino Brumidi. Below: Randolph Rogers's famous Columbus Doors, upon which each bronze panel features a different event in Christopher Columbus's life. Bottom: a closeup of the doors' bottom left panel, depicting Columbus on trial.

The National Statuary Hall is another popular attraction on visitors' tours of the Capitol. This hall was originally Benjamin Latrobe's Hall of the House. In 1864, it became a room to showcase bronze and marble statues honoring distinguished citizens from every state in the nation. Standing in the hall today are statues of such heroes as Utah's religious leader Brigham Young and Vermont's Revolutionary War hero Ethan Allen.

New members of Congress are sworn into office.

From its very beginnings, the Capitol has been a treasured national symbol. It is also where the daily work of the United States government is done. It is where our democratic ideals become reality. The Capitol is such an enduring symbol that many people and organizations ask to purchase the American flags that fly over the Capitol. To accommodate all the requests, employees of the Capitol's architect's office raise and lower thousands of flags each year for shipment. In one year, more than 97,000 flags were raised and lowered. That's about 268 flags a day! These flags are special simply because they have flown briefly over one of the most important buildings in U.S. history—the Capitol. Thomas Jefferson was correct two hundred years ago, when he predicted that the Capitol would captivate all who saw it.

GLOSSARY

architect – a person who designs and supervises the construction of buildings

Congress – the nation's lawmaking body; the legislative branch of government, which consists of the House of Representatives and the Senate

Constitution – the document that explains how the U.S. government works; written and signed in 1787 and ratified in 1788

foundation – the stone or concrete base upon which a building is constructed

House of Representatives – one of the two bodies of Congress; contains 435 members (large states have more representatives, and small states have fewer)

inauguration – the ceremony in which a government official takes the official oath of office; the president of the United States is inaugurated on the steps of the Capitol

Inauguration

renovate – to build additions or changes onto an existing structure

restoration – a construction project in which an old or damaged building is returned to its original condition

rotunda – a large, round room or building, usually covered by a dome

Senate – one of two houses of Congress; contains 100 members (two senators from every state)

Rotunda

Supreme Court – the highest court in the United States and head of the judiciary branch of government; the Court was housed in the Capitol until it moved to its own building in 1935

telegraph – electronic device invented by Samuel Morse that used a code to communicate messages over wire

TIMELINE

Construction begins on the Capitol

1787	U.S. Constitution signed
1790	Residence Act passed by Congress
1793	
1800	North Wing completed; Congress convenes
1803	Benjamin Latrobe appointed architect
1807	South Wing completed

War of 1812 { **1812**
1814 Capitol nearly destroyed by British troops

1824 Wooden dome completed

Construction of Capitol completed **1826**

1857 House of Representatives extension built

Senate extension built **1859**

1861

New dome completed **1863** } American Civil War

1865

Elevators installed in Capitol **1874**

Supreme Court moves out of Capitol and into new building **1935**

East Front of Capitol extended **1959**

1976

Capitol exterior restored **1987**

Old House, Senate, and Supreme Court chambers restored

INDEX (*Boldface* page numbers indicate illustrations.)

PHOTO CREDITS

Cover, Photri; 1, ©Cameramann; 2, Reuters/Bettmann; 3, Photri; 4, ©Brian Parker/Tom Stack and Associates; 5, Bettmann; 6, Photri; 7, North Wind Picture Archives; 8 (top), Bettmann; 8 (bottom), Library of Congress; 9 (top), Bettmann; 9 (bottom), Library of Congress; 10, 13, Bettmann; 14, AP/Wide World; 15, UPI/Bettmann; 16 (both pictures), North Wind; 17, AP/Wide World; 19 (both pictures), 20 (both pictures), Bettmann; 21, ©SuperStock; 22, ©Jon Feingersh/Tom Stack and Associates; 23 (top), Bettmann; 23 (bottom), AP/Wide World; 24, 25, 26 (left and bottom), Photri; 26 (top), 27 (bottom), ©Cameramann; 27 (top), Photri; 28, UPI/Bettmann; 29, ©Cameramann; 30 (top), Bettmann; 30 (bottom), North Wind; 31 (both pictures), Bettmann

ADDITIONAL PICTURE IDENTIFICATIONS

Page 2: *President Bill Clinton's inauguration ceremony, which took place on the steps of the Capitol on January 20, 1993*

EDITORIAL STAFF

Project Editor: Mark Friedman
Design & Electronic Composition: TJS Design
Photo Editor: Jan Izzo
Cornerstones of Freedom Logo: David Cunningham

ABOUT THE AUTHOR

Andrew Santella is a lifelong resident of Chicago. He is a graduate of Chicago's Loyola University, where he studied American Literature. He writes about history, sports, and popular culture for several magazines for young people.